Newbridge Discovery Links®

CLAY

VICKI TYLER WILT

Newbridge

A Haights Cross Communications Company

Clay
ISBN: 1-4007-3656-0

Program Author: Dr. Brenda Parkes, Literacy Expert
Content Reviewer: Nicholas Ruocco, Education, The Metropolitan Museum of Art,
New York, NY

Written by Vicki Tyler Wilt

Design Assistance by Kirchoff/Wohlberg, Inc.

Newbridge Educational Publishing
11 East 26th Street, New York, NY 10010
www.newbridgeonline.com

Cover Photograph: Clay pots
Table of Contents Photograph: Roofs of homes covered with clay tiles

Photo Credits
Cover: PictureNet/Corbis; Table of Contents page: Macduff Everton/Corbis; page 4: SuperStock; page 5:
(left) Index Stock Imagery, (right) Used with permission of Sterling Publishing Co., Inc., NY, NY from
NATURE CRAFTS FOR KIDS, ©1992 by Gwen Diehn & Terry Krautwurst, Photo by Evan Bracken,
a Sterling/Lark Book; page 6: James Robinson/Earth Scenes; page 7: Used with permission of Sterling
Publishing Co., Inc., NY, NY from CERAMICS FOR KIDS, ©2002 by Mary Elllis, Photo by Evan
Bracken, a Lark Book; page 8: Georg Gerster/Photo Researchers; page 9: (top left) Jehangir Gazdar/Woodfin
Camp & Associates, (top right) The Newark Museum/Art Resource, NY, (bottom left) CJ Collins/Photo
Researchers,(bottom right) Erich Lessing/Art Resource, NY; page 10: Alfred Ko/Corbis; page 11: Robert
Frerck/Woodfin Camp & Associates; page 12: Ken Heyman/Woodfin Camp & Associates; page 13: Farrell
Grehan/Photo Researchers; page 14: Rick Buettner/Bruce Coleman, Inc.; page 15: Michael S. Yamashita/
Corbis; page 16: Mike Yamashita/Woodfin Camp & Associates; page 17: (left) Brooks Walker/Envision, (right)
Kevin R. Morris/Corbis; page 18: Bernard and Catherine Desjeux/Corbis; page 19: Charles & Josette
Lenars/Corbis; page 20: Dallas and John Heaton/Corbis; page 21: Chris Hellier/Corbis; page 22: John Fulker

Illustration on page 21 by John Hovell

10 9 8 7 6 5 4 3 2

Guided Reading levels assigned by Newbridge, using the text characteristics
described by Fountas and Pinnell in *Guided Reading* (Heinemann, 1996).

TABLE OF CONTENTS

THE EVERYDAY WONDER

Here's a riddle for you.
Can you guess the answer?

It can be as soft as pudding or as hard as a rock.
You can write on it, carry things in it, or cook food in it.
You can make toys with it or build a house with it.

What is it?

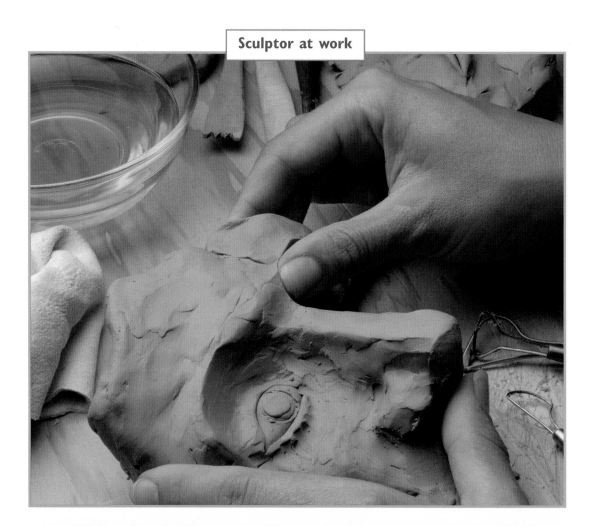

Sculptor at work

Handmade bowls

Flowerpots

The answer is clay. Clay is an important **natural resource** that can be found almost everywhere on Earth. For thousands of years, people all over the world have used clay to make useful and beautiful things. Today, we still use clay in many ways. What makes clay so special?

WHAT IS CLAY?

Clay is a kind of soil. It is made up of tiny bits, or particles, of rocks that have been ground down by wind and water for millions of years. When the particles mix with water from rain or from a river or lake, they form clay.

People mine kaolin, a special white clay that's used in making paper and pottery. This mine is in Georgia.

Wet clay is soft. You can roll it, mold it, or flatten it. What do you think these children are making?

Clay is special because when it is wet, you can squeeze it into any shape you want. The tiny particles slide around easily as you squeeze the clay. You can't do that with ordinary garden soil. It would just fall apart.

If you leave clay out in the air, it will harden and keep the shape you have given it. If you bake clay, it will get even harder. It will also become waterproof and fireproof.

This wonderful **material** can be used to make strong, lasting things, like pots for cooking or **bricks** for building. That's why clay is so special. And that's why clay has been important to people for thousands of years.

CLAY FROM THE PAST

People began using clay a long time ago. They dug it up from the ground and shaped it into pots. Inside the pots, people stored food and water. Sometimes they put the clay pots over a fire to cook food. The fire did not destroy the pots. In fact, it made them stronger. So people began baking their pots in fire to harden the clay. They made the first **pottery**.

Many of the pots that ancient potters made still exist. Scientists called **archaeologists** have dug up ancient pottery in places all over the world.

The pottery archaeologists find may be broken into hundreds of pieces. Putting a pot back together is like doing a puzzle!

Prehistoric toy ram from what is now Pakistan

Head rest, or "pillow," from China

Pottery is more than just pots. Lots of different things made of clay are called pottery. These pottery treasures were made long ago. What do they tell you about the people who used them?

Water pitchers from ancient Peru

Perfume holder from ancient Greece

AN ARMY MADE OF CLAY

One of the world's most amazing pottery treasures was discovered by accident. In 1974, some farmers in China were digging a well. Suddenly, they dug into a huge underground pit. Inside, they found more than 6,000 tall pottery soldiers lined up in rows! Two years later, archaeologists found another pit nearby. It contained about 1,400 more soldiers, lined up with their pottery horses.

This amazing clay army belonged to an emperor who ruled ancient China. The soldiers stand guard near the place where the emperor is buried.

Many of these clay soldiers are more than six feet tall!

This clay tablet is more than 3,000 years old. It was dug up in Turkey. The writing tells how two ancient kings decided to end their war and live in peace. A copy of the tablet hangs in the United Nations building in New York City.

STORIES WRITTEN IN CLAY

Long, long ago, people invented a way of writing. They cut their words into flat pieces of soft clay. Then they baked the clay so their words would last.

Archaeologists have found thousands of these clay tablets. The ancient language in which they were written does not exist anymore, but archaeologists figured out what the words mean. Some of the tablets tell what people sold to their neighbors in nearby towns. Other tablets tell the laws people obeyed or the stories they told.

WHEELS, KILNS, AND GLAZES

As you have read, pottery-making is a very old craft. The first potters did not have many tools for shaping clay. Sometimes they just made a hole in a lump of clay with their fingers to make a small pot. Another way they made pots is called **coiling**.

First, the potters pressed a lump of clay into a large, flat circle to make the bottom of the pot. Next they rolled pieces of clay into long ropes. Then they wound, or coiled, the ropes around the clay circle and upward until the pot was tall enough. Finally, they pinched the ropes together and put the pot into an open fire to harden the clay.

This girl is coiling pots the same way that ancient potters did thousands of years ago.

This pot is almost finished. Look at how smooth it is! Do you think a pot like this could be made by coiling?

ROUND AND ROUND

About 5,000 years ago, someone had a new idea for a way to make pottery. Why not put a lump of soft clay on a wheel? As the wheel spun around, potters could shape the clay more easily with their hands.

Early **potter's wheels** had a second wheel called a kickwheel, which the potter spun with a foot to make the main wheel turn. With the potter's wheel, people could work more quickly and make their pots smoother and more even. Today, kickwheels are still used, but most potter's wheels run by electricity.

INTO THE OVEN

The first potters put their pots into an open fire to harden the clay. Then, about 7,000 years ago, potters invented a better way to bake their pots. They made a special kind of oven called a **kiln**.

In some places, pottery is still baked in an open fire. Why do you think the heat is lower here than in a kiln?

These pots are red-hot! The temperature in a kiln can be more than 2,000°F. A kitchen oven only goes as high as 550°F.

The first kilns were made of clay, a good material to use because clay does not melt or burn. Potters could make a fire inside the oven. The pots sat on a clay floor that was raised above the fire. The smoke went out through a hole in the top of the kiln.

The clay walls kept the heat of the fire from escaping. That way, the inside of the kiln would get much hotter than an open fire. The higher the temperature, the harder a pot becomes.

This artist is painting a design on a vase that has already been glazed. He is using a special coating called enamel.

COLORFUL CLAY

Baked clay will hold water pretty well, but some of the water will leak out. Potters tried to find a way to make their pots more waterproof.

About 3,000 years ago, potters mixed sand, **minerals** from the earth, and water to make a coating for pottery. When the pot was dipped into the mixture and heated, the coating, or **glaze**, melted and turned glassy. Glaze kept the pots from leaking.

Potters added different minerals to glazes for color. Copper made green glaze. Cobalt made blue glaze.

Today, potters still use glazes to cover their pots and make them shiny and waterproof. The glazes turn bright colors when the pots are fired, or baked, in the kiln. Potters have many different colors to choose from to make their designs.

In this pottery shop in Kentucky, pots and dishes are made on a potter's wheel, and then decorated. What do you think this man is doing?

These pots look dull now, but they won't after they're fired. Each pot might be a different color!

BRICKS AND TILE

Ancient potters found another use for clay besides pottery. And they discovered it in an unusual way. After a river flooded, people noticed that some of the clay left behind would dry out in the sun and crack into hard blocks. The blocks gave potters an idea. Why not make their own clay blocks and use them to make buildings?

About 10,000 years ago, people made the first bricks. First, they mixed clay with water and straw. Then they pressed the soft mixture into molds to make blocks. Next, they left the blocks in the sun to dry and harden into bricks.

The people of ancient Iraq used sun-dried and kiln-fired bricks to build huge structures called ziggurats. Parts of this ziggurat are still standing after 4,000 years.

Builders stacked the bricks to make walls. As they worked, they spread a layer of wet clay between the bricks. When the clay dried, the bricks stuck together!

Many years later, people discovered a better way to hold bricks together. They used a cementlike material called **mortar**, which we still use today.

The Great Wall of China was one of the largest building projects in the world. It took hundreds of years to build and is more than 4,000 miles long. Parts of the wall are made of brick. Others are made of stone.

KILN-FIRED BRICKS

About 5,000 years ago, people decided to bake their clay bricks in the same kilns they used to make pottery. These new bricks were much stronger and could not be worn away by wind and rain.

Over the years, kiln-fired bricks became one of the most important building materials in the world. Bricks are fireproof and keep in heat, so people used them to build houses, stoves, fireplaces, and chimneys.

THE BEAUTY OF TILE

About 2,600 years ago, people began making thin, flat clay blocks called **tiles** to decorate walls. They also used tiles in roofs, floors, fireplaces, and stoves. People still use tiles to decorate their houses today.

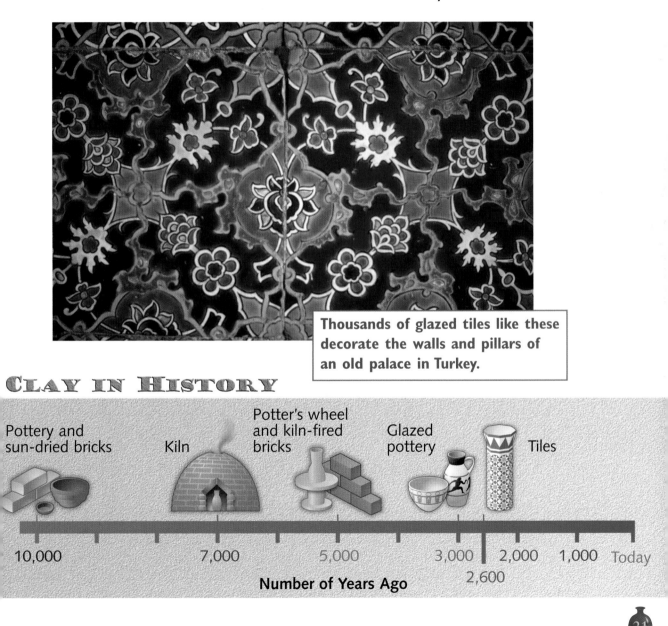

Thousands of glazed tiles like these decorate the walls and pillars of an old palace in Turkey.

CLAY IN HISTORY

Pottery and sun-dried bricks

Kiln

Potter's wheel and kiln-fired bricks

Glazed pottery

Tiles

Number of Years Ago

10,000   7,000   5,000   3,000   2,000   1,000   Today

2,600

CLAY IS ALL AROUND YOU

Take a look around your neighborhood, and you will see many things made of clay. Your home or school may be built of bricks. The walls of your bathroom may be covered with clay tiles. Your bathtub may be made of porcelain, a hard, shiny type of pottery. Inside your home, you may see plates, mugs, lamps, and decorations made of clay.

Clay from the earth has been used for so long and in so many different ways, it truly is a natural wonder!

We cook food in brick ovens today, just as people have done for thousands of years.

GLOSSARY

archaeologist: a scientist who digs up ancient objects and studies them to learn how people lived long ago

brick: a building block made of clay that has been dried in the sun or baked

coiling: a way of making clay pots by winding ropes of clay around a circle

glaze: a coating put on pottery to color it and make it waterproof

kiln: an oven for baking things made of clay

material: what a thing is made of

mineral: a natural substance that we usually get out of the ground, such as copper, iron, cobalt, or gold

mortar: a mixture that holds bricks together after it has dried

natural resource: a useful material found in nature, such as clay, wood, or oil, that helps people survive or improves their lives

potter's wheel: a machine with a spinning disk, or wheel, used to help shape clay

pottery: a clay object that has been shaped and then hardened by heat

tile: a thin, flat block of clay that is often glazed and used for decoration

INDEX

WEBSITE

To learn more about pottery, visit this Website:

www.artsmia.org/world-ceramics/